AUTHOR

Maggie Romanovich
Maggie Romanovich, APTD, is a trusted talent development advocate and advisor dedicated to fostering a culture of continuous learning and growth through professional development. She believes in embracing, developing, and amplifying strengths while aligning with strategic vision drives powerful results. She currently leads L&D efforts for national sales at Constellation Brands. The author's perspective is based on her experience and does not necessarily reflect Constellation Brands' training strategy.

Content Manager, Knowledge Management
Eliza Blanchard, APTD

Editor, *TD at Work*
Patty Gaul

Managing Editor
Joy Metcalf

Senior Graphic Designer
Shirley E.M. Raybuck

Peer learning is everywhere—whether via a business resource group in a formal work setting; through support organizations, such as those for new mothers; or in communities where individuals come together to learn more about the local area, religion, or leaders.

Industries have been built on peer learning. Just look at the rise of YouTube, Instagram, and TikTok stars teaching others how to apply makeup, change a dryer vent exhaust hose, put together the greatest seasoning, or learn a new dance. Instructors are joining the movement and uploading courses to popular learning platforms to share their expertise. When experts and curious individuals come together, they form peer networks.

Roughly 70 percent of learning comes from experience, 20 percent via peers, and 10 percent from formal programs. And as a learning leader, you can accelerate learning by formally organizing peer learning in the form of communities of practice (CoPs).

L&D professionals spend much of their time developing formal learning programs. Yet, in today's work environment where geographically dispersed workforces may limit in-person gatherings, many budgets are constrained, and the pace of business is increasing, you need to be intentional about fostering experiences and peer interactions to keep learning going. CoPs can help you do just that.

In this issue of *TD at Work*, I will:

- Review different peer learning methods.
- Highlight how CoPs work and their organizational benefits.
- Discuss methods of creating, maintaining, and encouraging CoPs.
- Outline best practices for successful CoPs.

Peer Learning Methods

Learning is in everything individuals do, both professionally and personally. People can choose to learn from any experience, and organizations have a responsibility to create environments where individuals can do and learn at the same time. You can facilitate those learning opportunities outside of formal learning programs in various ways. The following three means leverage organizational experts and peers but solve for different purposes.

Mentorships are relationships where a trusted guide counsels or influences individuals. An organization or talent development professional more specifically may facilitate this type of peer learning relationship when someone needs specific guidance for a set time period to advance or enhance knowledge or experience in a given area. The personalized direction develops the mentee while giving the mentor an opportunity to demonstrate coaching and leadership skills. This is typically a student-teacher relationship.

Project teams are goal-oriented groups tasked with achieving a time-bound assignment, often when a company defines a business need. The teams work to achieve that goal. This type of peer learning is a great opportunity for individuals to learn about new parts of the business and how different teams work together to accomplish an aligned business need. While being a member of a project team is beneficial from an experiential learning standpoint, the primary goal is not the learning but the achievement of the agreed-upon goal.

Communities of practice are groups of individuals who share a concern or a passion for something they do and want to learn how to do it better via regular interactions. Think of them as focused interest clubs that expand members' thinking around ways of working in an area of practice. CoPs enable experts to surface and exchange information, like a boiling pot where bubbles arise from different areas. You can use CoPs to amplify expertise and passion, elevating all members of the group. One week, an expert is a learner, and the next week that role may be reversed.

CoPs Defined

In 2002, Etienne Wenger, Richard McDermott, and William Snyder coined the phrase *community of practice* in their book *Cultivating Communities of Practice: A Guide to Managing Knowledge*. They used adult learning theory—specifically readiness—and self-concept to identify the partnerships that had initially been recognized in apprenticeship relationships. They discovered that these opt-in communities were everywhere, even when formal environments didn't exist.

> **Organizations have a responsibility to create environments where individuals can do and learn at the same time.**

CoPs extend learning beyond a formal learning program, enabling you to further help learners to improve, change, or amplify behavior. The communities can reinforce learning by commercializing organizational strategies, values, processes, and other concepts that are often your responsibility as the individual tasked to train others. When you can leverage organizational experience to demonstrate how to use a new tool successfully to change the workday in real time or troubleshoot a new process by putting it in the context of the work environment, you're extending that learning, engaging with employees, and sourcing new ways of modifying your training program.

However, just because individuals gather together does not make them a CoP. Departmental or cross-functional teams often briefly come together. By contrast, CoPs gather for long-term growth, development, and application in their respective fields. Three elements differentiate them from other group gatherings:

- **Domain.** This is the CoP's focus. It is a specific topic that is central to the group and is an area in which participants have high interest. The subject motivates and excites learners. Defining the domain helps you determine the terms and resources the group will use. Doing so also is vital to keeping the group focused, engaged, and motivated.

- **Practitioners.** As with other types of adult learning, immediate relevance is critical. CoPs should consist primarily of those who are practicing in the domain. That enables them to apply the shared learning in their everyday jobs and roles. Without the CoP being exclusionary, participants should be devoted to working in the respective space—not casually curious. For example, a CoP created around consumer insights should comprise those who are researching and developing insights every day or using them in their work. An accountant with a passing interest in consumer preferences should not join.

- **Community.** This encompasses interaction, trust, and communication. For a CoP to work, participants must trust each other and feel comfortable raising questions, providing answers, and sharing best practices. Community in this case in not about geographic proximity but rather about the rules and norms that members create that will help unite them. Interactivity is key. The intention with CoPs is not only to share but also to challenge, co-create, and exercise the concepts brought forth in the group.

CoPs can develop spontaneously or be formally organized. Spontaneous communities can develop out of shared interests discovered in an organized event. In the workplace, people can run into each other, start a conversation, and discover their common pursuits. Their curiosity sparks conversation, which leads to identifying a need to recruit like-minded individuals to share concepts and best practices and—more importantly—to think together to solve problems or things that stand in their way. Self-generated CoPs, which are organic in nature, ensure that participants' enthusiasm and motivation are baked into the group's formation, which leads to strong ownership and sustainability.

You may also see a need to establish a CoP around a specific topic. That will require more work to connect the appropriate individuals and create the group. But as a learning leader, you have the advantage of perspective. You have the opportunity to see when people are

---

Case Study: CoP Develops Organically

A company went through a reorganization that fragmented similar learning functions into interdependent units with different leadership silos. That led to a lack of clarity both on overarching strategies and resources that were available and applicable to the organization.

Solution: A group of learning practitioners generated a learning council to meet and communicate updates on a regular basis. The individuals saw an opportunity for better collaboration and began regular interactions among themselves. They share information once a month via virtual meetings; communicate regularly through email, text, and communication platforms; and have come together to generate new, cross-functional learning opportunities.

Results: This community of practice began as a place for individuals to share status updates, but it evolved into a professional development opportunity. The group's transparency and collaboration have increased, and the interdependent units now collaborate successfully. Further, the learning council and other practitioners come together frequently to engage in lively discussions about professional development via sharebacks and about best practices, self-paced learning evaluations, podcast and article reviews, and other skill-building activities.

struggling and where they are succeeding. Then you can step in and create an environment where individuals can gain exposure to each other and have discussions in a safe space to expand their way of thinking. For example, a unique way to consider using CoPs is in your onboarding program to provide context to the organizational vision, strategies, and processes. Create cohorts of new employees who can share how they're seeing the mission, vision, and values in action, and enlist veteran employees to act as guest speakers to share their experiences throughout the onboarding process.

Benefits

Experiential learning can have an incredible impact, and there are many reasons to encourage or create CoPs in your organization.

- Companies can leverage the knowledge that CoPs establish and use it to improve collective organizational intelligence. Encourage CoPs to commit to trying out new concepts or ways of working and then reporting their findings to the company during meetings or via messaging platforms.
- Crowdsourcing answers can help employees tackle challenges. Doing so gives them independence to find the answers they need, freeing up your time to focus on the bigger picture and other training priorities. Note: CoP members should have access to the individuals responsible for strategy execution so that those managers or leaders may validate and moderate conflicting ideas or nebulous solutions or help confirm strategy to ensure that the community is staying aligned with business goals.
- CoPs provide real-life application of the work employees are expected to do. It's one thing for companies to introduce a new process, tool, or procedure. It's another to have employees put it into action.
- CoPs can elevate the visibility of employees who are doers. Some may be eager to participate in an activity that highlights their expertise. You can also conduct an assessment on the domain, which can help you determine which employees have expertise on that topic. No matter how you land on the experts, once you have established the group, the CoP members

will have increased visibility among their peers, as well as with leaders. That can be a rewarding, motivating experience.

When organizations establish new processes, it takes time for employees to embrace those changes and integrate them into their daily work. As they integrate them, they will naturally adapt. You can use that adoption curve as an opportunity to learn and adjust new ways of working to make those modifications the realities of your workforce. When you not only observe how employees apply and modify or adjust the process but also take in that information to improve the process—which you can do via a CoP—you demonstrate how your employees' feedback mattered. That establishes trust, which leads to better collaboration and change adoption now and in the future.

How to Establish a CoP

Although CoPs may form spontaneously, in other instances, groups need encouragement to come together. If you are working with a geographically dispersed population that performs similar roles but in different departments and you see that they all have a drive to learn, it's worth encouraging them to come together as a CoP.

That said, for the group to be successful, participants must have open minds. CoPs enable people to learn from each other; however, individuals generally have their own established ways of working. With open minds, as CoP members are exposed to new approaches, they can adjust and improve. Learning new behaviors via experience enables the individuals to more quickly adapt to change, improves their confidence, and increases their competence. Individuals sharing successes and ways they effectively navigate challenges leads to more experimenting with their methods, increased education, calculated risk-taking, and learning from failure.

Before I delve further into how you establish and support CoPs, a note on your involvement: Depending on the participants, you may end up guiding the CoP or handing off responsibility to the community itself. In some cases, CoPs may be an extension of your learning programs and take the learning beyond the classroom, so you may want to guide the conversations. In other cases, practitioners may develop their own CoPs, and you may simply serve a consultant role, providing some structural support or guidance as they build their community.

Motivate Learners

Malcolm Knowles's adult learning theory stipulates there are six principles that contribute to successful knowledge transfer. For learners to participate and engage in a CoP, they must have a clear understanding of what's in it for them. If the value of the experience is not well defined, their effort will be short-lived.

When establishing a community, as with any other learning solution, demonstrate empathy toward the participants and determine the *what's in it for me* (WIIFM). When designing the community, use Knowles's six principles to motivate participants. If you can briefly address those six foundational adult learning needs, you will set up the CoP and participants for long-term success.

Relevance. They know why they are there learning and that it is important to their success and worth their time.

Self-concept. They are responsible adults who can manage themselves. They opt into the CoP because they understand the relevance. They know it is not mandatory. Rather, it is something for them to choose what and how they consume the content and interactions.

Learners' experience. They have a lot of existing knowledge that they want to refer to and lean on. For example,

they could be an expert presenter. The CoP's topic expands on something they want to learn more about.

Readiness to learn. They are confident the CoP will be relevant to their everyday work. They know they will come away with action items they can use immediately.

Problem orientation. They want to work with real-life examples, not theories and concepts. This is an action-oriented practice. They are not going to get mired in academics but in the steps they can take immediately that pertain to problems they face daily. They can contribute to the solution of these common challenges.

Intrinsic motivation. They want to participate on their own accord, not because they were told to. They know they will use this information and that it is a good use of their time. This will benefit them beyond checking an "I attended training" box.

Your organizational learning culture also plays a role in the CoP's success. Self-run communities tend to spring up in companies that do not necessarily value informal learning, whereas the more guided communities receive keen support for all learning types. Knowledge sharing varies as well. Where no structure or culture is in place, the sharing typically takes place in a siloed space rather than in the learning cultures where knowledge exchange is more centralized. While you are assessing and designing a CoP, ensure you are considering the company's learning culture and how it fits into learners' success.

Case Study: Talent Development Leader Initiates CoP

During an organizational needs assessment, a learning leader discovered that less-experienced employees frequently interrupted a handful of experienced workers to ask questions, leading to frustration and decreased productivity for the veteran employees.

Solution: The learning leader recommended establishing a community of practice for the less-experienced workers, where the experienced employees could share best practices, demonstrate ways to apply standardized tools and processes, and relay software tips and tricks through several modalities. The CoP would meet once a month in a live, virtual session while also employing a discussion board forum and centralized learning resources in between meetings.

Results: Participant engagement in the live sessions is high, individual contributors' visibility has increased, and new experts have emerged and opted in to be future presenters. Through this community, the learning leader can leverage the internal experience in this specialized function to elevate workers' collective knowledge, with the added benefit of saving money the leader may typically spend on hiring outside trainers to deliver that general knowledge. The internal experts and participants deliver and discuss the concepts in a directly applicable way.

Prepare

Start by defining your learning objective and identifying the domain, how the community will develop, and who the practitioners are. To lay out the potential learning topic or problem to solve, access needs assessments, notes from development conversations with learners or leaders, or a capability model (if your organization has an up-to-date one) that can give you the foundational skills for the CoP to focus on.

For example, a common training ask from managers is presentation skills for their team. After digging into a needs assessment, you likely will discover that team members have been through some type of presentation skills training course and instead need feedback and in-the-moment coaching. Rather than sitting in on every presentation their teams lead, managers could establish or their team members could join a CoP that is designed to be that opportunity for presenters to practice and develop their presentation muscles and where peers can coach each other to success.

Or perhaps the company's people managers are learning a new coaching model and want to talk through challenges and potential solutions before implementing the model with their teams. A CoP is a great place for them to do that and feel safe doing so. (See the template at the end of this issue with questions to consider about establishing a CoP.)

Gauge Interest

Next, set up an initial meeting with potential participants and gauge their interest in a CoP. If there's no interest, the group won't survive, and its genesis doesn't make sense. Refine the group's definition if its purpose is unclear while you are recruiting individuals. The idea is for the community to thrive independent of you, so ensure that the CoP has the energy to persist. This initial group could begin with natural leaders. Ask managers whom they often connect their people with. That could lead you to clear leaders in a given area.

Further, reach out to leadership and ask them to nominate experts. Then start the conversation with those individuals. Or if you have recently facilitated a benchmarking assessment, use that to determine an expertise threshold and source your group from those high performers.

When you gather prospective participants for that initial conversation, listen. In fact, do a lot of listening. When you ask the right questions, individuals will tell you what they're up against, what problems they need to solve, and which processes they need to work through. Collect and compile that information, then send it out to the group with a blueprint for connection. When facilitating the creation of CoPs, your role is to guide participants to a solution and clear the way for them to find it.

Create a Framework for Action

Once you have identified your initial group of participants, work with them to determine how they will operate as a CoP. You may need to provide guidance as the community gets started; alternatively, someone may rise to the occasion and take the lead. Regardless, setting a reliable framework and reinforcing its use enables the experts to focus on the content and activities rather than the act of organizing the participants. Keep these elements for your framework in mind:

Participation should be voluntary. When participants opt in, they are more willing to speak up and add value to the group. Be clear that the CoP needs all levels of expertise: seasoned veterans to offer advice and learn new ways of thinking and those new to the organization or new to their role who need that sage advice but can also offer fresh ideas because they are free from the constraints of habit.

Keep it simple. If you overcomplicate the process, the CoP will be difficult to maintain. Don't get in your own way. Set up ground rules for the community and have members agree on them.

Be inclusive. Focus on the practitioners, and be sure to include people who are new to but still practicing in the CoP's domain.

Encourage diversity of thought and open communication. Set the expectation that the CoP is open to all ideas. Don't allow people to squash each other's ideas. Challenge ideas and build on them.

Recap and summarize. Go beyond the brainstorm and do the work. Lay out the details and who is responsible for delivering them. Gather the pertinent information, such as what the domain is, who will lead each meeting, whether the group will recruit presenters or create a calendar of topics and discussions, how the CoP will recruit members, and how they will create a knowledge base and ensure participation.

Solicit input from members. Come prepared with general ideas, but encourage participants' early ownership and control in building the CoP. The group is meant for them to control—not you. Ensure the members rotate responsibilities, which distributes work evenly.

Mitigate concerns over conflicting information by identifying leaders who can quickly intervene or answer questions when the group generates conflicting or muddy answers. Ideally, those individuals will be in tune with the organization's standards and strategies to keep members on the right track.

In addition, set ground rules for idea sharing and collaboration. Empower members to redirect dominating participants, put digressions into a parking lot (but ensure they go back to them at a later time), and call on silent participants for new voices.

Cultivate Participation

Wenger and his colleagues have identified seven principles for cultivating communities. The principles foster a feeling of being alive that generates an excitement for participants and for the company, and that excitement sustains the CoP.

Ensure that there's a structure in place for the CoP to adapt over time. After you have established the community, ensure you cultivate the space for evolution. Many CoPs will develop out of an existing group, and the needs of that original group may change as business and time progresses. Encourage a growth mindset and inclusion.

Include a variety of perspectives. Bring in members outside the core community to advise on various subjects that are critical to the CoP's awareness and education.

Allow individuals to engage at different commitment levels. As a volunteer community, the group will have and should expect and embrace various participation levels. Some individuals will observe, come in where they can, take what they need, and leave the rest. Conversely, others will naturally step up, volunteer regularly, and take on leadership roles.

Encourage all levels of participation, because individuals learn in different ways. As the CoP evolves, members may rotate in and out of various participation levels. As Wenger, McDermott, and Snyder state eloquently, "To draw members into more active participation, successful communities build a fire in the center of the community that will draw people to its heat."

Open some conversations publicly but allow for private interactions. While the CoP will have a home base to discuss the important topics, ensure senior leadership is aware of the CoP's existence and the work the group is doing. You may recruit additional members this way or more guest participants.

Center activities on value brought to members and the organization. As your community develops, ensure you are discussing and sharing the value the community is providing to its practitioners as well as to the company. Make that a regular topic of conversation.

What are the outputs, and what does that mean to all involved? Establish methods for sharing that information with the entire organization through standard communication channels, such as team meetings, newsletters, and the intranet.

Establish expected routines while allowing for some spontaneity. Don't let the CoP get stagnant. Let the group's creativity flourish.

Keep your core objective in mind but encourage spontaneity and varied activities to keep engagement alive and healthy. For example, bring in a guest speaker who is superficially related to the domain to discuss a project she is working on. Play creativity-generating games to get new perspectives on problem solving. Plan an expo where the CoP highlights problems it has solved, and invite nonmembers to participate.

Set up a predictable and familiar cadence. By establishing routines for the CoP, you free up space for creativity in delivery, topics, and discussion. Set that cadence as your blueprint to enable the community to add color and texture.

Set Up Participants for Success

In a 2019 *Harvard Business Review* article, Francesca Gino discusses six tools that any group coming together needs to consider to truly collaborate versus engage in parallel play: Listen more than you speak, show empathy, practice giving feedback, understand the importance of leading as well as following, speak with precision, and engage in win-win conversations.

Although those principles are not directly tied to CoPs, guiding your participants through them will lead the group to better outcomes. Collaboration is critical to the community's success. Creating a sense of belonging opens up participants to sharing more and contributing to the team's collective elevation.

Gino also points out that "The task for leaders is to encourage an outward focus in everyone, challenging the tendency we all have to fixate on ourselves—what we'd

like to say and achieve—instead of what we can learn from others." As a learning professional, you are a leader who can cultivate open, trusting spaces for veteran practitioners to be vulnerable and new practitioners to ask the beginner-level questions, all without judgment. Setting up a safe space for candor leads the group to personal and professional growth.

Emboldening the CoP to embrace a challenger mindset pushes established boundaries and leads to expansive thinking. When participants leave their self-consciousness at the door, their universe of considerations opens to further exploration and discovery.

Set the ground rules at the group's origination so that expectations are clear. Revisit them from time to time and when new members join. It may be beneficial to commit them to a document and review them at the beginning of each gathering or to post them in a common area where anyone can review and remind themselves at any time.

When a group of solution-oriented thinkers choose to come together to increase collective knowledge, waste no time on nebulous communication. Commit to thoughtfulness, clarity, improvement, sharing, inclusion, and candor—then watch the CoP thrive.

Sustain Participation

Regardless of who is leading the CoP, the group must encourage discussion to be successful. It should do so through meetings, discussion boards, emails, newsletters, and other means. Encourage participation and generate excitement by developing a content calendar of topics for the group to cover. The further out the group plans, the more people will be ready and willing to participate.

Decide on the lead for each of the topics, and give those individuals a simple framework to work off of: Raise an issue or provide a theme, present a problem to solve together, and open the floor for discussion. It's that simple. Share the content and topic's resources with all participants, and ask expansive questions that build on the conversation.

As the group progresses, track participation. How many are in attendance? What is the average attendance rate? Are people participating during the

Virtual Engagement and Collaboration

Workforces are increasingly becoming geographically diverse, and more and more employees are working remotely. It is less common for employees to have a conversation around the coffee machine and discuss their shared interests. As such, one challenge you will face when organizing and encouraging communities of practice is enabling workers to engage virtually with each other. Foster opportunities for them to connect, and encourage them to reach out to one another and move beyond their comfort zones.

It's easy for employees to become distracted when working from home, especially when they are balancing work with their other personal responsibilities. Become a force of constructive disruption for CoPs and help them gain exposure to other people, ideas, ways of working, and parts of the company. Consider how you can recommend employees spend time developing.

First, many traditional live events—such as group discussions, panel discussions, pre-communicated questionnaires, and Q&A sessions—can still take place virtually, but keep in mind that the larger the group, the more likely participation will be limited during the event. Keep participants on mute and panelists on video and encourage participants to weigh in via the meeting platform's chat feature. Use messaging platforms to extend the conversation beyond the event.

For smaller groups, especially ones that are meeting to address focused topics, explore productivity tools that take communication beyond email, such as message boards, file sharing, and videoconferencing. Some of those tools even integrate with other programs so participants can find all the resources in one place.

Other social tools enable individuals to engage in quick chat-style communication and offer ways to establish specific focus area channels or groups. Many include hashtag identifications. Workspace sharing platforms allow for real-time collaboration and access to content. And don't overlook project management software, through which individuals can share action items, schedules, and other critical communication.

Regardless of the means and methods, it is imperative that you encourage and nurture CoPs to intentionally include others, build membership, and maintain their connectivity regardless of where individuals are working.

sessions? Make immediate adjustments. Ensure that the CoP's purpose continues and doesn't turn into a lecture series. Should you see that lecture environment setting in, meet with future presenters and help them find areas for group engagement.

Although you helped establish the CoP, consider ways to hand off responsibilities to a leader or individuals who rotate into that leadership role and run the CoP's administration.

Troubleshoot Issues

CoPs should be self-governing. In theory, when the group encounters an issue, the participants should work it out and create solutions that satisfy everyone. Sometimes a CoP's usefulness wanes and the community disbands. That doesn't mean the CoP was a failure. Perhaps the community established solutions that rendered its continued gatherings moot. Conversely, don't hang on to an unproductive use of time. Be aware of the following factors that can lead CoPs to lag.

Scope creep. When individuals meet regularly, there's a chance that the group's responsibilities could morph into project-based problem solving. Inevitability, issues may be raised that the group cannot solve. Additionally, if one person bears most of the responsibility of running the community, they could burn out, which could lead to the group's dissolution.

Solutions: Early in the process, define what participants should do when they suspect scope creep. Give members permission to speak up when they detect a shift in responsibilities. Assign someone to liaise with the appropriate stakeholders or responsible parties to accomplish the CoP's goals.

Establish your boundaries and maintain them. And have members share responsibilities in leadership to prevent overload.

Low participation. This occurs when the community stops adding value. Evaluate the group. It may be time to thank the group for its participation and move on. If not, examine why the participation is low.

Solutions: If the topics are stale or repetitive, if the same people are in the spotlight, or if the timing is off, identify ways to adjust. Additionally, look to recruit individuals who may be more casual practitioners. Open the CoP occasionally to those who are curious about the role or who want to add the domain to their own knowledge bank.

Overcomplication. Keep things simple. Don't require more from participants than they can give. CoPs should add value to their lives, not responsibility. When complications arise, empower members to speak up and redirect the group's focus.

Solution: Have members rely on each other to police complexity.

Mandates. Voluntary participation is at the CoP's core. As with any adult learning, intrinsic motivation drives participants to get the most out of their learning experience. Required participation is a buzzkill.

Solutions: Remind participants about the CoP's success and productivity rather than forcing them into a commitment they'll resent. Look into the cause of mandatory requirements and where they are coming from. If managers are pushing employees to attend, remind those leaders that the group's success relies on volunteerism and that they should use positive reinforcement to encourage participation. Further, ensure that participants and presenters have enough time to achieve their obligations; intervene if it gets to be too much.

Stagnation. If the group gets mired in the same routines, rehashes old topics, features the same experts repeatedly, or stops growing or rotating membership, it will get stale.

Solutions: Keep the meetings and discussions fresh and lively. If there are strong topics worth reviewing multiple times, make sure members are taking new approaches. Consider changing things up through different experts and presenters. Ensure that various participants find the spotlight. Be inclusive, and invite fresh perspectives and new members to the group.

Difficulty including new participants. When establishing the CoP, set up parameters for inviting new members into the fold. The CoP can be especially effective in onboarding new function specialists, because it gives them an opportunity to learn the cultural context of activities, concepts, and processes as well as how they're implemented in the real world.

Solutions: Make sure you're promoting the CoP. Members should share their successes with relevant audiences to raise awareness of the group so leaders can make appropriate recommendations to individuals who are new to their role or new to the company.

Encourage CoP members to pay attention for new practitioners to invite to the group. Include information about the CoPs in the onboarding materials you provide to new hires, and invite new employees to the meetings. If possible, also introduce the new hires in the meeting to welcome them to the organization and provide an extra sense of friendliness.

Leverage CoP Outputs

For L&D professionals, CoPs are a treasure trove of data for further development opportunities. They comprise engaged, self-driven learners sourcing their discussion topics from issues they are facing every day, identifying gaps in knowledge, and coming together to create solutions. If you are directly involved with the CoPs, obtain permission to build on the issues or gaps they struggle to solve.

If you are not, establish periodic check-ins to understand issues that come up frequently, and work to find what solutions you can help implement to close those gaps. As a center of excellence, cross-reference concerns, and find ways to combine efforts. Use the CoPs to source subject matter experts for future courses. Be open to group members' feedback, and find out where you can continue to improve your offerings.

Once you've established new areas to focus on, tap into experts to help develop structure for new courses, and include real-world uses for the content. You can also work with the community to validate or challenge hypotheses that leaders set that appear in your needs assessments and development conversations. If a topic comes up as an observed gap in capabilities, take that to the CoPs and ask participants about it. Perhaps employees have the knowledge, but the reason leaders don't see it is because of a systematic barrier that needs to be removed. Perhaps there's no accountability, so the activity is deprioritized. That provides a feedback loop for leadership that you can facilitate or empower the CoPs to communicate.

Measurement and Buy-In

As the CoPs develop and grow, it is critical that leadership supports them. Ideally, CoPs will meet during business hours with leaders' and people managers' support.

Ensure there is a clear definition of the CoPs to improve skills, performance, and morale and that the value of the groups is evident. Present a convincing case for leaders to encourage participation by measuring the community's effectiveness.

Start with your baseline by using the information you've collected to determine the need for the community in the first place. Take quick metrics of the practitioners' comfort and confidence level on the domains by requesting them to measure their thoughts using a Likert scale. Attach those to a numeric value and establish your baseline.

Periodically take stock of the participants' comfort and confidence, and establish trends in improvement throughout the CoPs' lifespan as well as relevance to their daily work, improvement in competence, and increases in participation. Use that information to share with leaders and to recruit members.

Also keep tabs on CoP members' participation in the meetings to reinforce the organic interest in the group and the various topics members discuss. Sometimes an attendance report or demonstration of participation increases or changes over time will tell a compelling story about the interest in the CoP.

Ask leaders periodically to identify whether they've observed improvement in their team's application of areas the CoPs cover. Be specific, and also be open to feedback and suggestions. The more information you can gather from participants and leaders, the more meaningful your community will be.

Share your results. As CoPs evolve, work with your communications teams to demonstrate the value the CoPs bring to the company. Inspire other communities to form and contribute to the organizational value.

Most companies have some level of executive or upper management sponsorship for their business (or employee) resource groups. The resource groups' objectives are to serve segments of the business and improve working conditions. Sponsorship is essential to elevate and champion ideas.

Just as a company would have a sponsor for the resource groups, you should have sponsors for CoPs, because the communities may identify an opportunity that could potentially require that level of organizational involvement. Perhaps the group identifies a software issue that requires funding for improvement, a need for additional staff, or other challenges that it can't solve alone. In those instances, the CoP will need an advocate with authority to help elevate concerns. That person may not be a regular member of the CoP but should be someone who has the group's best interests in mind.

Conclusion

In today's fast-paced environment, it's easy to fall back on traditional L&D methods. But experiential learning and peer learning are vital to employees' overall success, enabling them to expand on the skills they've learned in formal training programs. Leverage your strategic positioning to advise the company on providing structure to generate CoPs. These groups can foster enthusiasm and drive adoption of new concepts, processes, and procedures while troubleshooting challenge areas and hurdles via collective experience. Through CoPs, learners find new resources and inspiration for upskilling via resource sharing, mentoring, and peer coaching. Bring strategic partnerships to your organization by creating and nurturing a place of open-minded information sharing that benefits learners, the company, and you.

Books

Oberstein, S. 2020. *Troubleshooting for Trainers.* Alexandria, VA: ATD Press.

Wenger, E., R. McDermott, and W.M. Snyder. 2002. *Cultivating Communities of Practice: A Guide to Managing Knowledge.* Brighton, MA: Harvard Business Review Press.

Online Sources

Blankenship, S., and W.E.A. Ruona. 2007. "Professional Learning Communities and Communities of Practice: A Comparison of Models, Literature Review." Paper presented at the Academy of Human Resource Development International Research Conference in The Americas. Indianapolis, Indiana. Feb 28–March 4. files.eric.ed.gov/fulltext/ED504776.pdf.

Gino, F. 2019. "Cracking the Code of Sustained Collaboration." *Harvard Business Review,* November-December. hbr.org/2019/11/cracking-the-code-of -sustained-collaboration.

Gonçalves, L. 2020. "Communities of Practice: Everything You Need to Know." ADAPT Methodology, June 9. adaptmethodology.com/communities-of-practice.

Miller, A. 2020. "Creating Effective Professional Learning Communities." Edutopia, January 3. edutopia.org/ article/creating-effective-professional-learning -communities.

Pyrko, I., V. Dorfler, and C. Edin. 2016. "Thinking Together: What Makes Communities of Practice Work?" Sage Journals, journals.sagepub.com/doi/ full/10.1177/0018726716661040.

Wenger-Trayner, E., and B. Wenger-Trayner. 2015. "Communities of Practice a Brief Introduction." April 15. wenger-trayner.com/wp-content/uploads/2015/ 04/07-Brief-introduction-to-communities-of -practice.pdf.

Community of Practice Worksheet

Use this worksheet as a starting point for establishing a community of practice or advising individuals who want to start their own community.

Knowledge area: _____

_____

Business objective (What business objective does the CoP align to?): _____

_____

Initial topics (What information will the group discuss in the first four to six months?): _____

_____

_____

Prospective participants: _____

_____

_____

Practice (Do the participants practice within the domain?): _____

_____

_____

Leadership (Who will lead the group? How often will leadership rotate? Who are potential leaders who could serve as resources when conflicting messaging arises?): _____

_____

_____

New-member recruitment methods: _____

_____

_____

Cadence (How often will the group convene to discuss topics?): _____

_____

_____

Content sharing (Where will the group share critical information with each other? What meeting platform will the group use? How will the group share outputs and to whom?): _____

_____

_____

Commitment to community (What principles will the group follow to ensure success and inclusion?): _____

_____

_____

Additional notes: _____

_____

_____

Meeting Discussion Planning Template

Use this template—or share it with the community of practice leader—to plan out subtopics for discussions that fall in a CoP's domain for the group to address. Include the names of internal subject matter experts or outside leaders who will speak to the topic and when as well as how much time each will have.

Domain:	Presenter 1	Presenter 2	Month	Time Allotted (Minutes)	Additional Resources Required (Y/N)	Comments
Category 1:						
Subtopic 1:						
Subtopic 2:						
Subtopic 3:						
Category 2:						
Subtopic 1:						
Subtopic 2:						
Subtopic 3:						

Results Communication Template

Use this template to document a community of practice's success and then share the information with critical stakeholders.

What was the challenge or problem?

What are the business implications?

What solutions did the CoP discuss?

What worked? What didn't? Why?

What were the results?

What recommendations or solutions did the CoP develop?

Whom will the CoP recommend those to?	
Individual:	Leader:
Team:	Organization:

Who will make those recommendations? When?